THE DISRUPTIVE PHYSICIAN

THE DISRUPTIVE PHYSICIAN

HOW TO MANAGE THE CONSEQUENCES

OF BEING YOU

by Jacob DeLaRosa, M.D.

MISNER AND MONROE PUBLISHING

Misner and Monroe Publishing, First Edition 2017

Printed in the United States of America

Softbound:
ISBN-10: 0-9992632-0-X
ISBN-13: 978-0-9992632-0-4
Hardcover:
ISBN-10: 0-9992632-2-6
ISBN-13: 978-0-9992632-2-8
eBook:
ISBN-10: 0-9992632-1-8
ISBN-13: 978-0-9992632-1-1

Library of Congress Control Number: 2017911974

Book design by Morgan Crockett
Edited by Sandra Phillips

Acknowledgements

I dedicate this book to all healthcare providers who find themselves staring into the abyss. Have faith, there is light at the end of the tunnel.

To Melanie for being my rock. To Dan and John, the best teammates I could have. Dr. McBob for being a colleague and a bro. Juan and Julio mis hermanos. John P., Dr. Mark, and the Southern California Team. Jan, "No man a failure if he has friends."

Finally, to Mister and my amazing family (J-4, Giovanni, Donatella). No person can ever succeed without a strong family base.

TABLE OF CONTENTS

INTRODUCTION

I wrote this book to inform doctors and healthcare providers of what behavior can be classified as disruptive, and how easily a physician can be "labeled" and go down a path of doom!

I have found that many doctors don't realize that by simply being themselves, with no intent to cause harm, they stumble into an accusation of being termed "Disruptive."

During my tenure on the Medical Executive Committee, I found myself in the unenvious and often awkward role of judging my peers and also being 'judged'. I felt that this term, "disruptive physician" deserved deeper research. This issue is not one to be kept silent, but one to be brought out to be examined.

I began doing research to educate myself. After much effort I was able to identify the causes and how to correct disruptive behavior.

This book is designed to help you avoid exhibiting behavior that can be considered disruptive, and successfully navigate the process after an accusation has been made, or worse, if you have already been investigated and labeled disruptive.

This book is for you, the healthcare provider, who is required to go through any type of licensing board for behavioral issues; a medical physician, an osteopathic physician, a nurse, a physician assistant, a pharmacist or veterinarian, and for all who want to learn more about what it means to be labeled a disruptive physician.

This book is for the CEO, the medical staff office, and the Medical Executive Committee, to better understand physician behavior and how we are all affected.

After you have read this book, you will have a thorough understanding of what it means to be a disruptive physician. In addition, if you find yourself or others going down this path, this will be a guidebook to traverse the journey. I provide all the tools, resources, and information you need to succeed.

—*Jacob DeLaRosa, M.D.*

FOREWORD

I have received many calls from doctors facing a potential adverse action by a hospital. Too often, by the time they call me, the best opportunity to change the course of events has passed.

Alliances of friendship and collegiality with other professionals were never formed or have fallen apart. Warning signs flashed some months earlier, but went unheeded. Subsequent events have only put the doctor's privileges or employment at greater risk.

Against this backdrop, the value of advice in The Disruptive Physician, "How to Manage the Consequences of Being You" is critical to all health care professionals. Dr. DeLaRosa's information is a practical and educational call for doctors to examine the path they are on. The lesson is simple: The choices that help doctors avoid bad consequences are the same choices that help make them better doctors and better people.

If you practice being a better you, you can be you.

—Gregory J. Myers

Gregory J. Myers is a partner at Lockridge Grindal Nauen P.L.L.P. law firm in Minneapolis, Minn., where he practices in the areas of health care law and complex litigation. He has represented and advised numerous doctors in hospital administrative and disciplinary hearings and before state licensing boards—and has represented or advised many others that have avoided such hearings or resolved the underlying disputes.

CHAPTER ONE

A nurse called a doctor in the middle of the night. The nurse apologized for waking the doctor and informed him that she was concerned because one of his patients had not made any urine during her shift.

The doctor responded by hurling a barrage of profanity and insults at the nurse, finally informing her that the patient was in renal failure and, therefore, doesn't make urine.

The nurse apologized again to the doctor for disturbing him. The doctor hung up the phone without a response. The next day the doctor arrived at the hospital acting as if the previous night's conversation never happened, and proceeded to hand out donuts to the nursing staff.

What is Disruptive Physician Behavior?

According to an article in the *Journal of Medical Regulation*[1], "Disruptive physician behavior consists of a practice pattern of personality traits that interferes with the physician's effective clinical performance.

Manifestations are behavioral."

"The disruptive behaviors negatively impact the persons with whom the physician interacts. The behaviors include inappropriate anger or resentment, inappropriate words or actions directed toward another person, and inappropriate responses to patients' needs or staff requests."[2]

"The behaviors can be expressed directly to patients or indirectly through impeding the healthcare delivery team, or they may potentially compromise the quality of care of patients."

"A *Medical Staff Monthly* article cites case law that defines disruptive behavior as conduct that "disrupts the operation of the hospital, affects the ability of others to get their jobs done, creates a 'hostile work environment' for hospital employees or other physicians on the medical staff, or begins to interfere with the physician's own ability to practice competently."[3]

In its "Model Medical Staff Code of Conduct", the American Medical Association (AMA) defines inappropriate behavior as "conduct that is unwarranted and is reasonably interpreted to be demeaning or offensive. Persistent, repeated inappropriate behavior can become a form of harassment and thereby become disruptive, and subject to treatment as disruptive behavior".

The AMA defines disruptive behavior as "any abusive conduct, including sexual or other forms of harassment, or other forms of verbal or non-verbal conduct that harms or intimidates others to the extent that quality of care or patient safety could be compromised."[4]

An Extensive Problem

An article in the *Annals of Internal Medicine* states, "Our best estimate is that 3% to 5% of physicians present with a problem of disruptive behavior."[5] According to a survey in the *Physician Executive*, "More than 95% [of physician executives] reported regularly encountering disruptive physician behaviors, and 70% reported that the disruptive behaviors nearly always involved the same physicians. Disruptive physician behaviors most commonly involved conflict with a nurse or other allied health care staff. Nearly 80% of the respondents said that disruptive physician behavior is under-reported because of victim fear of reprisal or is only reported when a serious violation occurs."[6]

Consequences

According to The Joint Commission[7], *"Intimidating and disruptive behaviors can foster medical errors, contribute to poor patient satisfaction and to preventable adverse outcomes, increase the cost of care, and cause qualified clinicians, administrators and managers to seek new positions in more professional environments."* The impact of disruptive behavior on the healthcare organization can lead to:[8]

- Lowered staff morale
- Increased turnover of staff
- Undermined team effectiveness
- Poor patient satisfaction
- Negative reputation of the health care system
- Diminished patient care: medical errors, adverse elements
- Increased cost of care
- Lawsuits

While disruptive behavior can clearly have a negative impact on the medical practice or hospital, there is also a significant impact on the reputation, career and life of the physician who is accused or labeled disruptive: possible intervention, investigation, or professional and/or psychosexual evaluation, and consequences which may result in reporting conduct to the State Board of Medicine, and even potential termination or loss of privileges.

Prevention and Remedies

In 2009, The Joint Commission created a new Leadership standard to address disruptive and inappropriate behaviors, which requires healthcare organizations to develop behavioral standards, both positive and negative.

According to Reynolds in *The Journal of Medical Regulation*, "Keys to success in changing disruptive behavior involve a program of management that is intensive, multimodal, and long-term. Constructive change in disruptive physicians comes through requiring adherence to expected behaviors while providing educational and other supports to teach the physician new coping skills for achieving desired behaviors."[9]

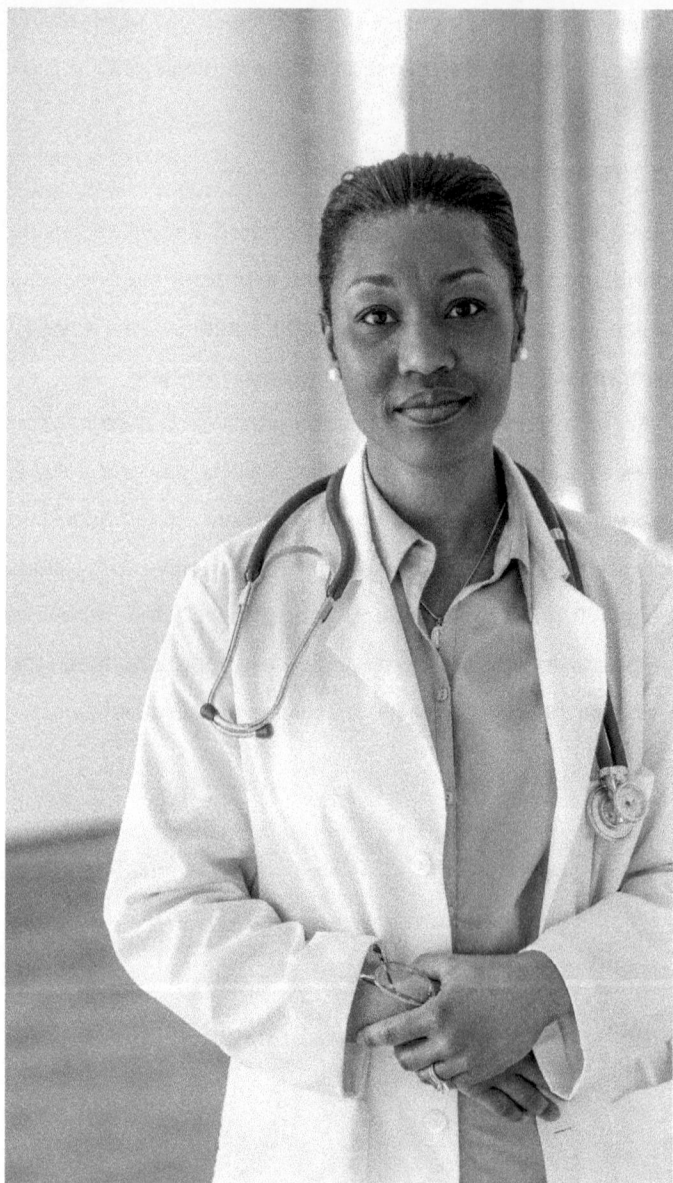

CHAPTER TWO

A NEW TERMINOLOGY:

GENDER BOUNDARY VS SEXUAL HARASSMENT

After a study session, a female medical student who lived a block away from where a male medical student lived, asked him if he could give her a ride home. He agreed. Subsequently, whenever the male student drove by her residence and noticed her, he would honk his car horn as a friendly "greeting".

Several months later, the Dean of the school called the male student into the office and accused him of sexually harassing the female student. The male student was labeled a "sexual predator". He became clinically depressed and was forced to seek therapy to resolve the issue.

A group of doctors were exiting a seminar on the topic of maternity. A lesbian doctor mentioned how badly she wanted to have a baby. One of the male doctors responded, "I have an hour available during lunch."

A male doctor passes a group of female nurses in the hall and calls out, "Hey guys, what's up?"

The terms "sexual harassment" and "psychosexual assessment" are often used in relation to disruptive behavior, and a physician can be classified as a disruptive physician if he or she engages in these types of acts.

Once the term sexual harassment is applied to someone, he or she is seen as a "bad person". The word "sexual" is used because we most often reference a male and a female. The term should be "gender boundary" when it relates to boundaries being crossed between genders, and in place of "psychosexual assessment" (which you will learn about later in the book), the term should be "gender boundary assessment".

Telling a physician, "Doctor, you have a sexual harassment problem" will most likely cause the accused to become defensive. Referring to the issue as a "gender boundary problem" allows the accused to be more receptive to engaging in a solution.

A gender boundary might manifest as simply, "I don't like the way you put your hand on my shoulder." That's not necessarily sexual. It's a gender boundary.

A gender boundary can exist between a male and a female, a man and a man, or a woman and a woman. We need to advance with the changes of LGBTQ and change this habit of using the term "sexual" because these issues can occur between any gender, and they are not always sexual in nature.

When the issue is related to treating someone differently and not related to sexuality, we should consider using the term "gender" and referring to the problem as a "gender boundary problem".

Gender boundary problems may relate to sensitivity about sexual stereotypes, sensitivity about gender stereotypes or anything that tends to be what someone feels uncomfortable with from another gender. So, currently, if somebody feels uncomfortable from the behavior of the opposite sex, then it's sexual harassment. If somebody feels uncomfortable from another gender, it's a gender boundary issue. This new term allows for gender neutrality. It's suitable for application to both male and female genders; it does not refer to one gender only.

For example, a doctor has a group, which is made up of six individuals (three women, one of which is a lesbian, and two men, including himself). The doctor treats the males in his group different than the way he treats the women. If a man asks, "Can you cover my call?" The doctor responds, "Not a problem." When one of the women asks, "Can you cover my call?" The doctor whines about it and makes a negative comment, causing the woman to feel uncomfortable about asking.

In today's terminology, that behavior could be classified as sexual harassment. I propose the term should be classified as a gender boundary, gender destruction, or a gender issue.

When we begin using the term "gender boundary", I believe people who have issues will be more open and receptive to change versus being labeled with a term that has a negative connotation.

CHAPTER THREE

| AM I A DISRUPTIVE PHYSICIAN?

A physician attended a child's birthday party at another doctor's house. At the party, which had young children in attendance, the physician witnessed one of the doctor's sons running around. He was hyperactive and disruptive—grabbing girls, lifting dresses, and engaging in inappropriate behavior.

The physician having the party suggested to the doctor that he have his son checked for attention deficit disorder as he had witnessed this behavior at other social gatherings and at his daughter's school.

The doctor became enraged. He was insulted that the physician would even suggest there could be an issue with his son. The physician apologized and never mentioned it again. Many years later, the doctor's son was diagnosed with a neurocognitive disorder.

According to Reynolds in *The Journal of Medical Regulation*, "Disruptive physicians lack closeness in relationships, lack empathy for others, and lack insight about their problem behaviors. They denigrate and resist mental health treatment."

"Pure disruptive behavior is motivated by the physician's need for power and control in relationships. Disruptive physicians seek to control others through intimidation. They are not team players. Invitations to act collegially meet with rebuffs. Disruptive physicians rebel against limits that are set on them."[10]

Reynolds further refers to the DSM-IV to note, "These individuals habitually resent, oppose, and resist demands to function at a level expected by others."[11]

Ouch! That seems like a harsh assessment, especially for a physician who has the best intentions and is often working under incredible stress with high stakes. Anyone can have a bad day and engage in an action or make an off-the-cuff remark that is misinterpreted.

The problem is, a moment of poor judgment or a misunderstanding can quickly lead to unintended and negative consequences. The best approach is to be proactive, do a self-assessment of your behavior, and take the necessary steps and actions to avoid becoming labeled a disruptive physician.

Self-Assessment to Determine If You Could Be Exhibiting Disruptive Behavior

If you exhibit *one or more of these behaviors*, it may be time to consider addressing the issue before it leads you down the path of an accusation. (This assessment and the following list is adapted in part from *The Journal of Medical Regulation.*[12])

- Yelling; verbal outbursts
- Foul and abusive language; profanity
- Threatening gestures
- Public criticism of coworkers
- Insults and shaming others
- Intimidation
- Invading one's space
- Throwing things or slamming down objects
- Physically aggressive or assaultive behavior
- Impatience with questions
- Hostile avoidance or the "cold shoulder" treatment
- Intentional miscommunication
- Unavailability for professional matters, e.g., not answering pages or delays in doing so
- Speaking in a low or muffled voice
- Condescending language or tone
- Engage in malicious gossip

- Racial, gender, sexual, or religious slurs or "jokes"
- "Jokes" about a person's personal appearance, e.g., fat, skinny, short, ugly
- Sarcasm
- Sexual harassment
- Being "touchy-feely" or hugging others
- Refusing to perform assigned tasks
- Continually "falling on your sword" or "dying on the cross"
- Being involved in other people's business or issues
- Disagreeing with the medical administration
- Implied threats, especially retribution for making complaints
- Refusing to perform assigned tasks
- Delays in performing assigned tasks (such as signing or delivering medical charts in a timely manner)

The following personality traits are most associated with disruptive physicians:

- Arrogant
- Intimidating
- Controlling; insistence of having things their way
- Inflexible, uncompromising

- Self-centered; exaggerated sense of self-importance
- Entitlement
- Un-empathetic
- Rationalize to justify their behavior
- Blame others
- Create upset and distress in others; viewed as difficult by others
- Denial; lacks self-awareness, insight, accurate self-appraisal
- Lacking in remorse; incapable of providing a genuine apology
- Failure to self-correct behavior
- Resists help
- Vindictive
- Litigious

"I'm Not Disruptive, But I Know Someone Who Is"

Before pointing fingers, remember when you're pointing fingers at someone else, you're pointing three back at yourself. If you review the self-assessment and determine "that's not me", then you don't have a problem.

If you review the self-assessment and conclude you know someone who does fit the description of a disruptive physician, the best strategy is to determine if the person is a friend or colleague with whom you can have a conversation.

If it is someone you can communicate with, then it's worth having an honest conversation to state how you see the person and discuss the different issues. How the person accepts what you tell them is not your responsibility. You will know that you did the best you could at that point. Your conscience will be clear.

If you witness disruptive behavior, when possible, I recommend you address the issue and say something to the person. If the person is not someone you can approach, refer it to that person's service line chief, or partner, or someone else on the medical executive committee who can address the issues. If you ignore the issue you're an accomplice in facilitating the behavior and allowing it to continue unchecked.

CHAPTER FOUR

BUT I AM A WOMAN, I AM IMMUNE TO

BEING LABELED A "DISRUPTIVE PHYSICIAN"

A very strong female general surgeon, well-liked by patients, who got the job done quickly, efficiently, and without complication, was working as a trauma surgeon on call. A trauma patient came in who was bleeding and needed emergency surgery. The operating room was cold, the patient was needing blood, and the female surgeon began throwing F-bombs left and right.

The patient survived and the surgeon thanked everyone for their assistance in the operating room. A few days later, however, one of the nurses complained that she was offended by the way the surgeon was using profanity in the operating room and the nurse felt uncomfortable while it was happening.

This led to an investigation which found that other techs and allied healthcare professionals also witnessed the surgeon swearing. Further, the investigation discovered it was common occurrence when the female surgeon was in the operating room.

Her name was then forwarded to the Medical Executive Committee, which asked the doctor about this behavior. The surgeon explained that in the heat of the moment she doesn't realize that she's doing these types of things.

She acknowledged that she did engage in this behavior but doesn't believe there is anything inappropriate about it because she grew up in a place where profanity was not considered derogatory toward anyone. The doctor declared she would not stop the profane language because it was never directed toward any one person.

The Medical Executive Committee informed her that if she didn't stop the behavior, she would be reprimanded and possibly lose her medical privileges at the hospital. The surgeon was offended. She did not understand how she could be labeled as disruptive when she wasn't hurting anyone and that, being a woman; she was immune to being labeled a disruptive physician.

According to a "Women in Medicine" report by AMN Healthcare[13], in 2015 female physicians made up 36% of the medical workplace, which will grow to an estimated 40% by 2018.

The largest percentages of women are focused in the areas identified below, with the highest number of women affected by the "disruptive physician" label concentrated in the areas of surgery:

SPECIALTY	PERCENT OF FEMALES IN 2015
Pediatrics	64.2%
OBSTETRICS & GYNECOLOGY	**56.7%**
Child Psychiatry	53.2%
Endocrinology	51.7%
Rheumatology	45.7%
Infectious Diseases	41.9%
Psychiatry	41.5%
Allergy & Immunology	41.5%
Family Practice	41.4%
Pathology–Anatomic/ Clinical	39.8%
Hematology / Oncology	38.9%
Internal Medicine	38.3%

Neurology	30.7%
Emergency Medicine	27.7%
Pulmonary Critical Care	26.8%
Diagnostic Radiology	26.6%
Ophthalmology	25.7%
ANESTHESIOLOGY	**25.6%**
GENERAL SURGERY	**21.3%**
Gastroenterology	17.8%
Otolaryngology	17.1%
CARDIOVASCULAR DISEASE	**14.4%**
VASCULAR SURGERY	**12.0%**
UROLOGICAL SURGERY	**8.7%**
ORTHOPEDIC SURGERY	**5.6%**

When we hear stories about disruptive behavior and sexual misconduct in the press, it's almost always about a man, but women are not immune to having this problem.

Women can be just as guilty as men in exhibiting disruptive behavior. Never think that because you're a woman you can't have a gender boundary, or you can't have an issue with professionalism, or you can't have an issue as a bully. A woman can be termed disruptive.

CHAPTER FIVE

HOW TO AVOID BEING LABELED

A DISRUPTIVE PHYSICIAN:

PROACTIVE STRATEGIES

TO PREVENT A PROBLEM

A doctor introduced a new PA who was working in the operating room and commented to a physician colleague who was present, "[This new PA] is visiting here from out of town, could you hook him up with some people while he's here?" The physician colleague responded to the new PA, "Oh, I know a couple ladies. Do you mind having some transgender people?" Of course, that is not what the doctor meant by "hook him up with some people."

The doctor immediately discussed the conversation with the PA, telling him "I meant no offense by my colleague trying to set you up with some people to meet while you're here. All I meant was that you don't know anyone in this city and could he introduce you to some friends to meet for dinner. By no way did I mean to try to insinuate that you needed to date someone, be it male, female or someone whose transgender. I hope you were not offended?" Fortunately, the PA laughed and said it was all okay.

The previous chapter provided an extensive list of examples of disruptive behavior to assist you in assessing your own personality to determine if the "consequences of being you" may lead to a label as a disruptive physician.

If you recognized yourself in any of the disruptive behavior examples, this chapter is designed to help you avoid being accused and investigated by offering proactive strategies you can implement to prevent a problem before it develops.

Communication is the First Key

A physician once told a surgeon a story that when he was a student he had a classmate who exhibited inappropriate behavior. As a student, he felt his classmate sexually abused him. The surgeon asked,

"How did he sexually abuse you?" The physician told the surgeon, "In the emergency room he would rub my ear, or hit my ear, or he'd rub up behind me, and I felt very uncomfortable. It was very upsetting. I informed someone at the school and they did nothing about what happened."

Ten years elapsed, and the physician saw his previous classmate again, which brought back emotional memories about the abuse he suffered. Now the physician is in therapy to deal with the trauma of the experience.

The surgeon asked the physician about when he saw the classmate again, "Did you confront him?" The physician responded, "No. I'm still uncomfortable about it." The physician asked, "Do you think perhaps he didn't even know that what he was doing made you feel uncomfortable?" The physician was quick to answer, "Oh no, he knew what he did because he did it to other people as well."

What if the classmate didn't even know what he was doing was offending his classmate? For example, if every time I walk by a nurse named Laura and say, "Hey Luke and Laura, what up? "Luke and Laura". Hey, "Luke and Laura", and Laura is thinking, "God, that pisses me off so much", but Laura never says anything to me, then how am I to know my behavior makes her uncomfortable? We all know someone whose personality is "over the top", and we may assume they're aware of their own behavior, yet often they may have no awareness of their own behavior or how it impacts others.

All along, I thought Laura actually liked the reference to Luke and Laura from *General Hospital*. I never had any clue that what I was doing was tormenting her because it reminds her of the *General Hospital* days of the ice princess, and she was called the Ice princess, and it has affected her entire life.

The first key to resolving an issue, or preventing an issue before it arises, is communication. There can be a lot of misunderstanding just because of the way staff or colleagues communicate.

The story about the PA, which began this chapter, is a perfect example of how something that was intended as an innocent statement and goodwill gesture, could have quickly turned into an offensive conversation that made someone feel uncomfortable, but through communication it was resolved.

It's imperative to clearly communicate and to clarify what the intention is in the things we say and the things we do. You can say and intend one thing and another person may interpret it completely different.

A doctor asked a nurse, who he had known for a long time and who had just been promoted from a clerk to a registered nurse, "Is anyone backing you up?" She responded, "Excuse me?"

So, the doctor asked again, "Is anybody backing you up with this sick patient? The patient is very sick and it's not fair that you, as a new graduate, are here already taking care of these very sick patients without any backup." She answered, "No. I'm okay." The doctor's response was, "Well, if you need anything, let me know."

The nurse reported the conversation to the administration who informed the doctor that the nurse felt humiliated, belittled, and insulted by what he said to her. What the doctor had meant by his question to her is that it's not fair that she was new and she didn't have a resource backing her up. The nurse interpreted the doctor's comments to mean that he thought she was so incompetent she couldn't take care of patients by herself.

What I recommend is (1) never give unsolicited comments, and (2) if you do give unsolicited comments, you better clarify your comment—explain exactly what you mean in clear terms.

Even this happens to me:

Several years ago a surgeon that relocated from Alaska to Idaho stopped to meet with me on his way through town. He explained that he was coming into an area of Idaho that the existing surgeons where not collegial or friendly to him coming to the same city. As he explained to me his situation I took him in with open arms as I felt it was unfair to ostracize or to treat anyone in such a manner. I remember when I first came to town and was treated the same by the existing group. He came with his significant other and I toured them around the hospital, the facility and showed them the new hybrid operating room which was being built from the ground up at the hospital. I explained to the surgeon that this was the first true hybrid operating room being built west of the Mississippi. We parted ways and I looked forward to seeing him in the near future.

A few years went by and I heard that the surgeon was doing locums coverage at a nearby hospital. I reached out to him to say hello and he answered that he was tied up with something currently and he would get back to me. He never returned my call.

Another year or two went by and this doctor was in Portland, Oregon as a proctor for a new procedure that a surgeon in the area was doing. An old colleague and friend went to dinner with this surgeon and commented on how she used to work in Idaho. The surgeon asked where and with whom and she told him with me. He went on a tirade and commented on how she could have worked with me as my ego was so big! He went on to tell her that I had the gall to tell him that, "I was the best surgeon west of the Mississippi." My friend went on to tell the surgeon that he must have the wrong person because that does not sound like something that Dr. DeLaRosa would ever say!

Meeting this surgeon years earlier I thought we got along so well and I was looking forward to working with him. What he took away from our meeting was that I was an arrogant prick! He had heard and interpreted something completely different than what I had said.

For years he has been thinking ill of me from our first and only meeting on what he interpreted I said. I should've been clear in my comments and my follow up and not offered unsolicited comments. It is easy to see how one can be interpreted so wrong and leave such a bad taste with another when only trying to be kind.

Be Aware of the Power Differential When Communicating

While it would have been best if the nurse in the previous story had simply confronted the doctor during the conversation and asked for clarification, it is possible she felt too intimidated.

It's important for physicians to remember that there is a *power differential* between a physician and a nurse, a physician and a tech, a physician and a worker, and any person in the hospital. The power differential might have influenced the nurse to feel it was not a safe environment for her to ask a question.

Anyone in a power position, meaning that when there is a power differential—be it a man or woman—wherever you sit in the hierarchy when there's a power differential, you have the capacity to be in the position of being unprofessional or having a behavioral issue. It does not matter how nice you are, or well intentioned.

The person in the power position will be deemed responsible for causing the problems. If you get into your car and allow someone else to drive, and there is an accident, who is responsible for the accident? Is it the passenger or the driver? The driver is responsible. The driver of the car is the one who is going to be responsible for causing the problems.

As physicians, we must be vigilant about how we communicate with people when there is a power differential. When we're working, we're professionals. In our communication, we must always be professional in what we're discussing. In many businesses people are friendly with one another and may talk about all kinds of personal things, like family and what's going on in their life.

When there is a significant power differential between physicians and others, I believe "friendly personal" discussions should be avoided in the hospital setting. If there is something to be undertaken outside the hospital, that is your decision and your prerogative to make relationships outside the hospital. But while in the hospital, we can never forget that there is truly a power differential between physicians and others that work in the hospital, and we cannot waver from professionalism while we're dealing with others.

Determine Why You Engage in
Disruptive Behavior

Everything we think, everything we feel, and every action we take has an underlying subconscious reason behind it.

If someone says, "You look great today", your response may be, "Thank you" or you might reply, "Oh no. No, I don't". Why did the person make the statement to you that you look great? Consciously, the person may have said it because you do look great. But what is the person's subconscious saying?

The subconscious reason for saying it is that the person may want you to like him or her, and he may want you to think he's a good guy or gal, because it's important to him or her at an emotional level to be liked and thought of as a good person.

Even the response of, "Oh no, no I don't", has a hidden meaning behind it. Consciously, the "receiver" of the compliment may think "It's no big deal, I don't really look special today", but subconsciously the receiver may not like being noticed, and being recognized for how he or she physically look makes the receiver feel uncomfortable.

What is the real reason behind what you are saying or doing? There is always a fear or desire behind every statement and action.

Using the "Solution to Change the Behavior Worksheet" included at the end of this chapter, note the disruptive behavior you wish to change. Next, identify the fear or desire that causes you to engage in that behavior. Then express what you believe will happen, in other words what the negative consequences will be, if you were to experience the thing that you fear or if you experience your desire not being met.

EXAMPLE

What is the disruptive behavior I wish to change?	*I want to stop being "touchy-feely" with patients and staff at the hospital.*
What is the fear (or desire) behind the behavior?	*I touch people because I want them to like me and think I'm a warm, nice person (or I touch people because I'm afraid people won't like me and think I'm cold and not empathetic).*

What do I believe will happen (the consequences) if I experience the thing I fear (or if my desire is not met)?	*If people don't like me or think I'm not a nice person, they might complain about me, and I could lose patients or be fired. Ultimately, if I'm fired, I'll have difficulty acquiring another position, I'll lose money, I won't be able to pay my mortgage, my significant other will leave me, and I'll never see my kids again, etc...*

Uncovering the underlying fear or desire which leads you to engage in the disruptive behavior may be challenging. Freud believed that all our actions are a result of childhood experiences. Often you will need to **"peel through many layers of the onion"** to locate the cause at the core. As you peel that onion to find out why you think, feel and act the way you do, you'll discover that the onion will go all the way back to childhood.

The discovery process may be difficult to explore on your own, and you may wish to consider working with a qualified therapist. Below are three more tools to assist you in "peeling-the-onion".

LIFE TIMELINE

Life experiences, and specifically childhood experiences, condition and program our behavior. Complete the "Life

Timeline Template" included at the end of this chapter, which notes the major events in your life by age, to help you reveal what life experiences may be causing you to engage in disruptive behavior and to uncover the core fear or desire that drives it.

For example:

A 13 year old child was in 8th grade, and applied to attend a private high school where all his friends would be attending. The child wasn't accepted to the private high school. That experience for the child, at the time, was devastating.

This imprinted a feeling within that, "I'm going to show you [everyone who did attend the school] that I will be better than you." This feeling drove the child to be successful in everything tried.

It also programmed into the child's subconscious that it is important to be liked by people, and to never be considered a phony, because at the core of the onion (due to the child not being accepted at the preferred private high school), the child feared not being good enough.

In medicine, fear could possibly manifest as yelling at hospital staff. It could drive a physician to engage in that type of disruptive behavior and justify the behavior of yelling as a concern for patient care. But what's really behind that behavior? They fear being considered a fraud; they fear the consequence of a complication or even a lawsuit.

GENOME TREE

A Genome Tree is used to identify patterns. On a blank piece of paper, draw a "tree" of circles or squares with arrows or "branches" springing forth that identify the members of your family. Place yourself in the middle, surrounded by your parents and siblings.

Then move to the next level with your grandparents, uncles, aunts and cousins, and so forth. Select your behavior issues, such as a pattern of being loud and abrasive or being "touch feely", being an alcoholic or having anxiety disorders, etc. Now identify those people in your family who also exhibit that behavior. This is simply another technique that allows you to discover where the behavior originated.

INCIDENT ASSESSMENT

An Incident Assessment (included at the end of this chapter) is used to notate each incident of disruptive behavior and identify why it happened, where you may have been at fault or responsible, and what you could have done different, so you can be aware of, and change, your behavior patterns in the future.

THE "CULTURAL EXCUSE"

Someone who engages in disruptive behavior may use the excuse that it's normal based on his or her culture. It's simply the way the entire culture behaves. While it may be true, and it's not necessary to judge it as bad or good or place blame on anyone, the fact is, wherever you are, you must understand the culture you're operating within.

Is it appropriate to engage in the behavior in your current environment? If it's not, then you either need to relocate to an appropriate environment or change your behavior.

One doctor is acquainted with a neurosurgeon who is very loud, macho, boisterous and yells all the time— at everybody! He is very abrasive and makes the staff uncomfortable. The doctor asked the neurosurgeon what the problem was, "Why do you yell all the time?"

His response was that it's a cultural thing and very normal within his family, "My father is Puerto Rican, and every time he spoke, he'd just yell. He was just loud. He's mad at the car because it's broken and he yells at the car. Then you're talking to him and he yells at you." The whole time the neurosurgeon was telling the doctor this story, he was yelling at the doctor!

Is his heart in a bad place? No, not at all. But he is a disruptive physician and he needs to address the issue and make the decision to either change his environment or change his behavior before he damages his career.

Identify What Triggers Your Behavior

Now you're going to identify what triggers your behavior. What types of situations, comments, or actions catapult you into engaging in disruptive behavior? When you are aware of your triggers, you can anticipate them and devise a plan to avoid relapse. Fill in the 'Triggers' section in the "Solution to Change the Behavior Worksheet" for each behavior you wish to change.

For example:

A neurosurgeon who was not allowed to wear his white coat inside of the operating room area would wear it whenever he left to get coffee. A doctor suggested to him he make a habit of leaving his white coat at the hospital so he didn't accidently wear it outside of the allowed area.

His response was, "It really pisses me off when I'm driving and I see a guy standing there with the orange vest on holding a stop sign and he demands I stop. What gives this guy, who probably only makes $15 an hour, the right to tell me to stop? Who gives him the authority to be my boss? I'm a freaking neurosurgeon! Now someone in the hospital is telling me what to do? Who the hell is that person to tell me what to do? Don't you agree?"

The doctor calmly answered, "Maybe the guy in the orange vest is doing it because he's trying to help you by preventing you from driving your car into a ditch. Perhaps the hospital employee is trying to help you by preventing you from making a mistake or infecting someone." The neurosurgeon refused to see that perspective.

What triggers him is anyone whom he deems as "beneath his status" telling him what to do. That triggers him to become angry and to do the exact opposite action. Why does he do this? When he was a child, he grew up a poor foreigner from Greece and was bullied by other kids.

So now, when he sees someone who he considers lower than his social class tell him what to do, he associates that person with the bullies from his youth, and it triggers that old emotional pain of not feeling good enough because he was not born in America and he was considered a "nobody".

He fears being seen or judged as a "nobody" and being told what to do. He believes the consequences of allowing someone to tell him what to do makes him appear weak and an easy target to be bullied. He justifies engaging in the disruptive behavior because he believes, by refusing to follow orders, he is protecting himself by making it known he is not a poor "nobody" who can be bullied.

Change Your Behavior

Once you understand why you engage in disruptive behavior, and identify what triggers the behavior, you can resolve and change the behavior through your new awareness and approach of the way you think, feel, and respond to the trigger.

Below are tools to support you in implementing changes.

TOOL #1: ACCEPTANCE

In the book *Stages of Change*, James Prochaska and Carlo DiClemente write about the pre-contemplation stage, which is denial.

The pre-contemplation stage is followed by the contemplation stage, which is when a person becomes aware and accepting. Acceptance is the first step on the road to change.

It may be difficult to engage in acceptance when you're the person who is in the wrong, but it is imperative to do so in order for change to take place.

TOOL #2: MAKE A COMMITTED DECISION TO CHANGE

The question is: Do you want to continue to engage in disruptive behavior? If your answer is no, then a committed decision must be made to change.

"Committed" is another term for "dedicated". A committed decision means you will do whatever is required to make the change, no matter how difficult or challenging the shift. You are declaring your desire to change is stronger than any fear.

Once you decide you no longer wish to live the way you have been living, define how you do want to live and the new person you want to be.

TOOL #3: THROW OUT SHAME AND ABANDON THE BAD

Shame is when you feel less than others. Shame has no purpose. If you've been ashamed, you must remove the shame. Understand that mistakes are human and you can move on.

When you feel ashamed because you have wronged someone, and you have attempted to make it right by speaking with the person, and the person is unaccepting of your apology, you must move on and get past it. If you don't move on from shame it will continue to be a problem in your life.

A much respected surgeon volunteered to undergo a 360-evaluation from nurses and medical staff. The surgeon was very charismatic and had no worries that his 360-evaluation would be excellent. Heck, he was the go to surgeon when anyone in the hospital was sick and requested by almost all of the employees and medical staff.

When the results came back of his 360-evaluation he was dumfounded. The evaluation said the surgeon was arrogant, lacked empathy, cocky, and treated women that are pretty different than women who were not. The surgeon was presented with this information and he was disappointed and said he was "ashamed" of himself. The surgeon went on for the next few weeks feeling bad and sorry for himself. He wondered who could have written such shameful comments and how he was a failure. The surgeon thought long and hard about therapy to confront these issues. His first lesson on his road to recovery was to stop feeling shame!

The surgeon realized we all make mistakes and when we do we learn, get better and move on. The surgeon was given a gift that very few get. Honest unabated comments on oneself and the ability to improve. Once shame was removed from his person he was able to start the healing process to improve himself.

TOOL #4: TAKE RESPONSIBILITY AND MAKE AMENDS

It's important to take responsibility for how your actions affected others and, when possible, make amends to those people who were adversely impacted by your behavior.

TOOL #5: TRUST IN A HIGHER POWER

Regardless of your spiritual beliefs or non-beliefs, you may find the tenants of *The 12-Step Program*, specifically trusting in a Higher Power, to be useful in maintaining strength during challenging times.

TOOL #6: SUPPORT GROUP OR SPONSOR

There are numerous support groups available which offer the opportunity to connect and meet with other physicians who may have similar experiences. You might also consider gathering with a group of trusted colleagues in a safe environment, which allows you to honestly and openly discuss issues with one another. Also, you can find yourself a sponsor. A sponsor is someone you can trust to talk with who will give you honest answers not just what you want to hear.

TOOL #7: BE AN ACTIVE OBSERVER

Many people benefit from having their own vigilant "observer"; the "you inside of you" who acts as an observer on your shoulder. It's the little voice that can say to you, "Hold on. Do not be in this room with this nurse by yourself. Hold on. Don't talk about other physicians or other people. Hold on. Stop talking about what you did last night." Use your observer as your guide.

TOOL #8: HAVE A PLAN TO CHANGE THE WAY YOU RESPOND TO YOUR TRIGGER

We change our response (how we act or behave) to a trigger by changing how we think about the trigger and how we feel, emotionally, about the trigger.

As you notice a thought or feeling being "triggered" by a situation, event or comment, consider, "How can I now think about that differently and feel about that differently so that I don't exhibit the negative action or engage in the disruptive behavior?" Have a plan to deal with a trigger before it is activated. To assist you with this exercise, complete the "Solution to Change the Behavior Worksheet" included in this chapter.

Trigger	Distressed when you don't spend time with your family.
Disruptive Behavior	Fail to deliver charts on time.
Solution	Attend to fewer patients. Learn better time management. Schedule, on the calendar, an hour each day to complete the charts. Set a daily alarm as a reminder to work on the charts.

Trigger	Patients are not out of bed by 9:00 am.
Disruptive Behavior	Raise your voice at the nurse.
Solution	Schedule a meeting with the nurse to explain your concerns, and why it's important for the patients to be out of bed by 9:00 am. Involve the nurse in the care of the patients.

Trigger	Engaging with patients and staff.
Disruptive Behavior	Hug and touch everybody.
Solution	Envision a hula-hoop between yourself and everyone who is not your family. Consciously maintain the "hula-hoop distance" between yourself and others. Implement the "smell test": If you can smell the other person, you're too close.

TOOL #9: ADOPT A NEW SET OF PRINCIPLES AND SET BOUNDARIES

Identify and list your values or principles—for example, honesty, trust, faith, integrity, courage, justice, perseverance, loyalty, and hard work. Now, place an imaginary fence post (which is made up of your values). That fence represents your boundaries. You do not go outside of your fence and you do not allow anyone inside the perimeter of your fence unless they share the same values or principles. This tool helps protect both you and others.

A Note on Substance Abuse and Dependencies...

Substance abuse, addictions, chemical dependencies and drug use are outside the scope of the content of this book. If you discover your disruptive behavior is triggered by a dependency or addiction—be it drug abuse, alcohol, pharmacology from medications, sex addiction, etc.—I encourage you to proactively seek help. Visit my website at **TheDisruptivePhysician.com** for more information and resources to assist you.

Worksheet: Solution to Change the Behavior

THE BEHAVIOR
What is the behavior I want to change?

THE FEAR OR DESIRE THAT CAUSES THE BEHAVIOR
What is the fear (or desire) behind the behavior?

THE CONSEQUENCES
What do I believe will happen if I experience the thing I fear (or if my desire is not met)?

TRIGGERS
What situations, comments, or actions trigger the behavior?

THE SOLUTION
What is the new belief I will adopt, and the new action I will implement, to change the behavior?

Template: Life Timeline

AGE	SIGNIFICANT EVENT	WHAT FEAR OR DESIRE DID THIS EXPERIENCE CREATE?

Worksheet: Incident Assessment

DISRUPTIVE BEHAVIOR INCIDENT	
WHY DID THIS HAPPEN?	
WHERE WAS I AT FAULT?	
WHAT COULD I HAVE DONE DIFFERENTLY?	

DISRUPTIVE BEHAVIOR INCIDENT	
WHY DID THIS HAPPEN?	
WHERE WAS I AT FAULT?	
WHAT COULD I HAVE DONE DIFFERENTLY?	

Worksheet: Principles & Boundaries

MY PRINCIPLE/VALUE	MY BOUNDARY

Reference: The 12 Steps

STEP 1: POWERLESSNESS

Admit I am powerless over my behavior and that my life has become unmanageable.

STEP 2: HOPE

Believe that a Power greater than myself can restore me to sanity.

STEP 3: SURRENDER

Make a decision to turn my will and my life over to the care of a Higher Power, as I understood that Higher Power.

STEP 4: INVENTORY

Make a searching and fearless moral inventory of myself.

STEP 5: CONFESSION

Admit to a Higher Power, to myself and to another human being the exact nature of my wrongs.

STEP 6: READINESS

Ready myself to have a Higher Power remove all my defects of character.

STEP 7: ASKED A HIGHER POWER

Humbly ask a Power greater than myself to remove my shortcomings.

STEP 8: AMENDS LIST

Make a list of all persons I have harmed, and become willing to make amends to them all.

STEP 9: MAKE AMENDS

Make direct amends to such people wherever possible, except when to do so would injure them or others.

STEP 10: CONTINUE INVENTORY

Continue to take personal inventory and when I am wrong promptly admit it.

STEP 11: KEEP CONTACT

Seek through prayer and meditation to improve my conscious contact with a Higher Power as I understood that Higher Power, praying only for knowledge of that Higher Power's will for me and the power to carry it out.

STEP 12: HELP OTHERS

Experience a spiritual awakening as the result of these steps, and try to carry this message to others, and to practice these principles in all my affairs.

(Adapted from the original 12 Steps of Alcoholics Anonymous)

CHAPTER SIX

I'VE BEEN ACCUSED OF BEING
A DISRUPTIVE PHYSICIAN, NOW WHAT?

Being accused of disruptive behavior may cause feelings of anger, fear, or defensiveness. This is a natural response. Take a deep breath and keep an open mind. Often, a first-time accusation can be quickly and painlessly resolved.

Every hospital has policies and procedures in place for dealing with incidents and complaints. If an accusation has been made against you to the Medical Executive Committee (MEC), the first step they will take is to refer to the bylaws for direction.

Following the Bylaws

As you are part of the hospital and are credentialed in that hospital to work, you function through the bylaws. Though similar, everyone's bylaws are distinct, and it is important that you have knowledge and understanding of the bylaws in which you operate.

Most bylaws encourage the use of progressive steps to be taken by medical staff leaders and center management, which begin with a collegial intervention and educational efforts to address those questions relating to an individual's clinical practice and/or professional conduct. The goal of these efforts is to arrive on a voluntary responsive action by the individual to resolve questions that have been raised.

Collegial Intervention: What to Expect

Often, the first action taken when an accusation is made is to conduct a prompt collegial intervention. The physician will be called into a formal meeting, which will be led by a respected peer. You may or may not be notified of the purpose of the meeting prior to the intervention.

During the meeting, you will be advised about the policies regarding appropriate behavior and about your obligations as a physician. The discussion may include proctoring, monitoring, consultation, and guidance. The peer may share relevant information, as well as other clinical protocol guidelines, to assist a person in conforming his or her practice to appropriate norms. The intervention will be documented and documentation included in all relevant files.

The physician will be notified of the accusation. The peer may reveal the specific event or may choose to share non-specific information to protect the accuser. The physician will then be given the opportunity to respond to the accusation. The physician's response will be documented by the person doing the intervention.

Usually, a collegial intervention does not include specific corrective action or a monitoring period, it's simply a warning, "Hey, listen, you need to watch out. These are the things you do, here's how you can improve upon your behavior and get better."

TIPS FOR A SUCCESSFUL COLLEGIAL INTERVENTION

- The collegial intervention is a time to listen. It's a time to absorb. It is not a time to come back with guns blazing and denials. It's a time of just listening and taking account of what is being said.

- Remember, your actions and words will be documented in a report that the person doing the collegial intervention will share with the Wellness Committee or Medical Executive Committee.

- If you are not prepared to deliver a verbal response to the accusation during the meeting, consider putting your response in writing after the meeting has concluded. Make a simple request, such as, "I'd like to process this information and put my response in writing."

- Do not become angry, hostile or defensive during the meeting.

- Do not ask the identity of the accuser.

- Do not retaliate against the accuser.

- Do not attempt to change the subject or try to deflect the topic.

- Do not blame or yell at the person conducting the intervention. Remember, your peer is trying to help you.

- Once the meeting has completed, document in writing the content of the discussion. In the event the situation escalates, you, or your lawyer, may wish to refer to your notes on the conversation.

- Ask the person conducting the intervention if she or he has any tips on how you can avoid this behavior in the future. Ask for help. "Do you have any recommendations to avoid this type of problem in the future?"

- Complete the conversation on a positive note. Appreciate and acknowledge having the collegial intervention with you, "I appreciate you having this collegial intervention with me."

Acceptance

Your acceptance or denial of the collegial intervention can determine the rest of your career—and your life.

Acceptance means, regardless of if you believe the behavior was appropriate or inappropriate, you accept that someone was impacted or felt harmed. By choosing acceptance, you agree you can improve your behavior and you are open-minded to the possibilities. You approach the issue as a glass half full versus half empty. You see the experience as a life lesson and an opportunity to be a better person.

ACCEPTANCE: THE STORY OF A SUCCESSFUL COLLEGIAL INTERVENTION

A physician and director engaged in casual small-talk, the physician noted the appearance of a woman in the director's office and asked if one of the other doctors was "messing around" with her. Both men laughed, and the director responded, "I don't know."

Later, the physician was called into a collegial intervention meeting with one of the senior physicians. The director had expressed concerns; how he felt uncomfortable by the physician's remarks and was placed in an awkward position and didn't know how to respond or what to do.

The physician immediately acknowledged the conversation and apologized, stating he in no way meant to insult the director or the woman. He recognized that this "locker room" conversation was not professional, and thanked the senior physician for bringing the inappropriate behavior to his attention. He took responsibility and promised it would never happen again. No further actions were taken. That is a successful collegial intervention.

ACCEPTANCE RESULTS

- Collegial Intervention
- Do the recommendations
- Issue resolved
- Successful

Denial

Denial is exhibited through excuses, deflecting, blame, and incredulous behavior, "I'm not accepting this. I'm pissed off. I'm going to fight this because I don't believe I did anything wrong."

Consider that if one person makes an accusation or observation it may not be true. If two people accuse you, they may be colluding. But if three people notice the same behavior, you better do a self-assessment.

If you don't accept the collegial intervention and you continue the same kind of pattern of disruptive behavior, the situation will escalate and the next step will be an investigation.

DENIAL: THE STORY OF AN UNSUCCESSFUL COLLEGIAL INTERVENTION

A surgeon continued to use a tool that was previously banned by The Joint Commission (formerly the Joint Commission on Accreditation of Health Organizations or JCAHO).

During a procedure on a patient, the surgeon was informed by the director of the operating room—who was a nurse—that he could not use the tool. The surgeon became enraged, and yelled at the nurse. The incident was reported to the Medical Executive Committee.

A collegial intervention was conducted with the surgeon, where he was informed that he could not use the tool, nor could he yell at a nurse who was simply doing her job. The surgeon refused to comply, stating "This was how I was trained to perform procedures, the ban is wrong and it's not the way it should be done."

The Medical Executive Committee referred the issue to the Wellness Committee who conducted an investigation. The surgeon maintained his position that he was right and the hospital was wrong to expect him to change.

The surgeon's stance forced the Wellness Committee to implement corrective actions, which included a course on professionalism. The surgeon refused to attend.

The MEC gave the surgeon an ultimatum: comply with the corrective actions or have his privileges removed. The surgeon would not budge. Instead, he left the hospital and searched in vain for employment elsewhere.

This is a sad example of an unsuccessful collegial intervention; unsuccessful simply because the surgeon refused to accept responsibility and change his behavior.

DENIAL RESULTS

- Collegial Intervention
- Do NOT do the recommendations

- Issue NOT resolved
- Consequences / Unsuccessful

Being Investigated

An unsuccessful collegial intervention often results in an official investigation. The criteria for initiating and conducting an investigation should be outlined in one's respective bylaws.

An example of common bylaws related to investigations could read, "Any person can provide information to the Medical Executive Committee about the conduct, performance, or competence of medical staff members. A request for an investigation or action against a medical staff member may be initiated by the medical staff president, CEO, or the Medical Executive Committee."

Below are some potential ways of investigating:

POTENTIAL INVESTIGATORS

The investigation may be conducted by:

- A colleague
- An ad-hoc committee set up specifically to investigate the accusation
- An external peer-review consultant
- Medical staff peer-review
- The Wellness Committee

- The Medical Executive Committee
- An independent party within the hospital
- An outside entity, such as an attorney

COMPONENTS OF THE INVESTIGATION

The investigation may consist of:

- Interview with the person who filed the complaint
- Interview with the accused physician
- Interviews with the physician's peers and staff
- Corroboration of complaint by other witnesses
- Review of surveillance video (if relevant)
- Review of computer records (if relevant)

TIPS FOR A SUCCESSFUL INVESTIGATION

- Cooperate
- Be forthright and honest
- Maintain good behavior
- Know your bylaws and your contract
- Do not leave the hospital

CHOOSING TO LEAVE THE HOSPITAL TO AVOID AN INVESTIGATION

I recommend you do not leave the hospital in an attempt to avoid an investigation. Once an investigation has been set, it will be reported to the National Practitioner Data Bank (NPDB) if you leave your hospital during an investigation.

You will experience trouble acquiring a state license as well as getting credentials in another hospital, because one of the questions a new hospital will ask is, "Have you ever left a facility because of a pending investigation?"

The decision to leave the hospital prior to, or during, an investigation will follow you for the rest of your career with negative consequences.

Results of the Investigation

Once the investigation is complete, the Medical Executive Committee will review the material, formulate a conclusion and make a recommendation. The results of a hospital investigation are peer protected, while the results of an employer investigation may be discoverable and not protected by law. If an investigation is conducted by an attorney "in anticipation of litigation" (i.e., there is an accusation of unlawful harassment, etc.), that investigation very well may be confidential and protected by the attorney-client privilege.

INVESTIGATION CONCLUSIONS
AND RECOMMENDATIONS

The investigation may conclude that the physician is not disruptive and therefore, no action is required. The investigation may conclude the doctor has exhibited bad behavior or poor judgement but the incident is a first-time offense and doesn't rise to the level of being labeled a disruptive physician, and therefore, the recommendation consists of a warning or limited corrective action, such as a one-day course on professionalism.

Or the investigation may conclude the doctor is disruptive and is considered a liability to the hospital, which could result in a recommendation of moderate to severe corrective action, and even removal of privileges. Recommendations vary and are guided by the bylaws.

CONCLUSION	POTENTIAL RECOMMENDATION
Not Disruptive	No action is required
Exhibited Bad Behavior	Warning and/or limited correction action is required
Disruptive	Corrective action is required

REPORTING THE INVESTIGATION CONCLUSIONS AND RECOMMENDATIONS

The results or conclusions of the investigation may be reported to:

- The board of the hospital
- The State Medical Board
- Authorities (such as the police, federal agents, or local authorities) in the case of an illegal offense such as sexual assault

POTENTIAL CORRECTIVE ACTIONS

Corrective actions are dictated by your bylaws, and may include:

- Action may be deferred for a reasonable time when the circumstances warrant
- Therapy or course for professionalism
- Issued a letter
- An admonition censure
- Reprimand
- Warning
- Probation
- Special limitations
- Restriction, modification, suspension, or removal of clinical privileges
- Reduction in physician's staff privileges
- Suspension

- Evaluation
- Termination
- Loss of privileges

Options When Receiving an Unfavorable Recommendation

If the investigation concludes that you are a disruptive physician and you receive an unfavorable recommendation, you still have options. An unfavorable recommendation is an action that has significant adverse impact on your career, and threatens your ability to practice medicine. It could be any of the following actions:

- Sent for An Evaluation
- Suspension or Probation
- Loss of Privileges
- Termination

KNOW YOUR CONTRACT AND BYLAWS

Know what actions or behaviors your contract states are considered "termination for cause" and "termination without cause". Many physicians have only looked at their contract one time, when they were signing it. Some have never read it. Now is the time to fully review your contract and bylaws.

INITIATE A NOTICE OF HEARING

Your bylaws may grant you the right to initiate a notice of hearing. *(Of note, each and everyone's own bylaws are different and you must know what is in your hospitals bylaws.)* When you receive an unfavorable recommendation in regards to clinical competence and professional conduct, then a hearing can be triggered.

Refer to your bylaws for specific requirements and details. Common bylaws provide that once you request a hearing, there will be a 30-day period following the date of receipt of such notice.

A panel may be convened and evidence presented. Once the hearing is completed a judgement will be rendered.

In most cases, the burden of proof is on the physician who initiated the hearing. Most panels will recommend in favor of the Medical Executive Committee or the Board unless it finds that the individual who requested the hearing has proved with a preponderance of evidence that the recommendation which prompted the hearing was arbitrary, capricious, or appears to be unfounded or not supported by credible evidence.

APPEAL TO THE HOSPITAL BOARD

If you are unsatisfied with the outcome of the hearing, you can always appeal to the Board of the hospital. Most bylaws will define this process. It is common that the grounds for an appeal are limited, and usually require a substantial failure to comply with a fair hearing plan.

The final decision of the board is often provided within 30 days after the receipt of the review panel's recommendations.

LAWYER UP!

Hire an attorney so you know your options. At any time during this process, you can acquire a lawyer. Select a lawyer who is familiar with hospital law, Medical Executive Committee law, hospital contracts, medical staff bylaws, hospital bylaws, and medical staff issues. The American Medical Association (AMA) has a list of attorneys who specialize in healthcare law. Attorney costs may range from $150.00 an hour to up to as high as $1,500.00 an hour depending on your geographic location.

WAYS AN ATTORNEY CAN HELP YOU

- Writing responses to letters you received
- Formulating answers to questions you are asked
- Acting as a sounding board; someone who can

brainstorm with you, and present ideas and options

TIPS FOR HIRING A LAWYER

- Ask the attorney if he or she has previously dealt with the issue of disruptive behavior or accusations of unprofessionalism or sexual harassment in the healthcare industry.

- Inquire about the attorney's track record with the above issues. What results have they achieved?

- If possible, negotiate for a fixed cost versus an hourly fee.

- Select an attorney who is even-keeled and supports your goal; someone who presents the options to you, but is always leaning toward working things out and achieving your ultimate goal (which might be to leave the hospital, or stay in the hospital, or have your name cleared, etc.)

- Avoid hiring a lawyer who wants to come out with both guns blazing; someone who wants to file numerous motions or an injunction or conduct a countersuit will create a bigger challenge than trying to work the issues out. Hospitals have more money and more resources than you. Quoting Benjamin Franklin, "You catch more flies with honey than you do with vinegar."

CHAPTER SEVEN

I'VE BEEN LABELED A DISRUPTIVE PHYSICIAN:
THE PSYCHIATRIC AND PSYCHOSEXUAL
EVALUATION PROCESS

If you have an unsuccessful collegial intervention, followed by a subsequent investigation which concludes you are a disruptive physician and the recommendation is to send you for a Psychiatric evaluation, you may feel like you've just been catapulted into hell. This chapter is designed to guide you through the evaluation process so you can successfully walk out the other side.

A disruptive physician evaluation (also known as a professional evaluation) or a psychosexual evaluation (which is recommended if any type of issues of boundaries with the opposite sex are involved), includes the evaluation of the behavior, an executive summary which covers the evaluation findings and diagnosis, and finally concludes with a recommendation for next steps and actions.

According to Reynolds in *The Journal of Medical Regulation*, a "professional evaluation serves as a guide to developing a program of remediation and monitoring as a benchmark against which to measure future change."[14]

COMPONENTS OF AN EVALUATION MAY INCLUDE:

- Physical history
- Physical exam
- Psychological evaluation
- Psychiatric history
- Sexual history (psychosexual evaluation)
- Addiction history (if relevant)
- Collection of collateral information

- Social history
- Treatment history
- Mental status evaluation
- Behavioral observation
- Drug test
- Polygraph exam

Selecting an Evaluation Center

The hospital will provide a list of approved evaluation centers and instruct you to secure an appointment within a specified time-period. Once you have secured the appointment, you will need to inform the hospital so they can forward your file to the clinic.

The evaluation process may last three to five days, from 8:00 am until 5:00 pm each day. You will most likely be responsible for the cost of the evaluation, as well as your travel and accommodations, which can range from $6,000 up to $10,000.

NATIONALLY-KNOWN CENTERS

- Scottsdale Behavioral Health & Wellness Institute **(623-414-2978)**
- Seasons in Malibu **(424-610-5402)**
- Professional Renewal Center **(785-842-9772)**
- New Orleans Center for Mind-Body Health **(504-355-0509)**
- Betty Ford Foundation **(310-307-7053)**
- Promises Treatment Center in Santa Monica **(310-695-1708)**
- Pine Grove Behavioral Health and Addictions **(888-574-4673)**
- See the *Resources* section for additional information

Preparing for the Evaluation

The best way to prepare for the evaluation is to understand the purpose of the process. You are paying a clinic to assess your behavior of an accusation or the results of an investigation made against you. Your initial interaction with an evaluation center will be with a salesperson who is selling you on purchasing their service.

They may seem friendly and nice, but they are a salesperson with the goal of making a sale. At the end of the day, they represent the evaluation clinic and the hospital that has made allegations against you. They do not represent you. They have no interest in helping you. They are like car salesmen.

Physicians and healthcare providers that have gone through this process warn to be vigilant and conscious of the fact that you are treated as you have a deep problem and any objective testing that will be done in the evaluation center the validity will be questioned. An abstract written by Greg Futral a licensed psychologist and Dr. James "Jes" Montgomery from Pine Grove Behavioral Health and Addiction Services in Hattiesburg, MS reported that in psychological assessment data of healthcare professionals presenting for evaluation they commonly produced questionable validity results due to social desirability concerns.[15] Understanding what you are about to do and how your results are viewed will make you better positioned once the evaluation process commences as well as several steps ahead of many other physicians who have traveled this road before you. Understanding what you are going to face makes all the difference in the world. The unknown is difficult to understand and brings apprehension. Following are a few more tips to help you successfully navigate the process.

Plan to Bring a Support Person to the Evaluation Location. Every night after the evaluation you will return to the hotel alone. This may be a difficult or lonely time for you. It's always great to have a confidante with whom you can talk. Consider bringing someone with you who is supportive of you, such as a spouse, significant other, colleague, family member or friend.

Plan to Maintain an Exercise Regimen During the Evaluation Process. This can be a challenging process and you may feel mentally drained and emotionally exhausted after each day of sitting for long periods of time for interviews. Consider packing gear to exercise or selecting a hotel that includes a gym so you can maintain physical fitness.

Prepare a List of People for Collateral Information. During the evaluation process, collateral information will be gathered from other people who may include your coworkers and people outside of the hospital, such as your spouse or family. During the admitting process at the evaluation center, you will be asked to provide a list of names of people who can provide collateral information, and consent to contact them. Prior to providing the list, be sure to inform anyone who may be contacted by the evaluators.

The hospital will also provide to the evaluation center a list of people to contact for collateral information. The people on the hospital's collateral information list can only be contacted upon your authorization.

If there is anyone on the list you do not want contacted, you may withhold your authorization. However, your refusal to give consent to contact the person will be noted in the executive summary of the evaluation.

Be cooperative as possible regarding consents, but don't shoot yourself in the foot by approving someone who has a vendetta against you or who you believe may not maintain confidentiality.

Day One of the Evaluation

Upon arrival for your evaluation, the administration will make a copy of your driver's license or other form of identification; collect the remainder of your payment if they haven't collected already. Note that if you change your mind and decide not to go through the evaluation, your money is not refunded. The administration will ask you to sign documents and waivers agreeing to the evaluation process. You will then undergo a series of exams, which may include:

- Physical exam conducted by a nurse practitioner
- Laboratory and blood samples
- Hair samples
- Urine sample (with an observer)
- IQ test (Color Repeatable Battery for the Assessment of Neuropsychological Status Update)
- Personality Assessment Inventory (PAI)
- The Million Clinical Multiaxial Inventory-IV (MCMI-IV)
- The Paulhus Deception Scale (PDS)
- Substance Abuse Subtle Screening Inventory-3 (SASSI-3)
- Boundary Violation Index (BVI)
- Sexual Addiction Screening Test Revised (SASR)
- Etc.

After lunch, which is on your own, you will be assigned two people, usually a therapist and a PhD, who will be interviewing you and gathering information for the evaluation. Day one will conclude around four or five o'clock in the evening.

Request a Copy of Your Results

You must request a copy of your results in order to receive your evaluation report with the executive summary and recommendation. During the intake process, be sure to complete the form that allows you to receive the results. You will be asked to provide authorization to release the information to third parties—be it the board of medicine, your hospital or employer, etc.—don't forget to give consent to yourself!

Day Two of the Evaluation

Day two of the evaluation begins with more questions from a psychiatrist or an addictionologist. Following this interview, you will meet with another psychologist about boundary issues. After lunch, you will have a four-hour meeting with your primary psychologist. You will be asked the same questions repeatedly to determine if there are any variations in your answers.

QUESTIONS MAY INCLUDE:

- When was the first time you had sex?
- Do people consider you arrogant?
- When was the first time you masturbated?
- Do you watch pornography?

- Do you engage in sexting?
- Do you treat people who you find attractive different than others?

Be Professional and Be Yourself

When you're sent for an evaluation, physicians that have participated in these evaluations assert that there is an assumption by the evaluators that you are guilty of an offense and it is their job to uncover it and to prove it. During the process, do not focus on trying to prove your innocence, simply be yourself. The evaluation is not intended to prove if you are guilty or not. Remember, you are not "the doctor" anymore! The evaluators are not your friends. They're not going to have coffee with you afterward. Their job is to assess your behavior and judge you. Every action, comment and behavior will be noted in their summary. They are professionals that primarily deal with behavioral issues and report on what they assess.

Final Day of the Evaluation

At the completion of the day, your psychologist will discuss their findings and recommendations. Day three of the evaluation will dictate if you will undergo a polygraph if you are only present for a Psychiatric evaluation. If you are undergoing a psychosexual evaluation you need to plan for a polygraph. At the end of your meetings on day two, the psychologist will forewarn you on the questions that will be asked, which are usually four specific questions. In addition, he or she will ask you one last time, "Is there anything else that you want to say about why you are getting the evaluation?"

The Polygraph Exam

The polygraph exam is usually conducted by a professional. Often, he or she will be a former law enforcement officer or federal agent. Physicians that have been through this process state that the examiner will inform you, in depth, how proficient he is as an examiner, how he has solved major cases using polygraphs, how the machine is never inaccurate, and that it has a 99% chance of catching you in a lie.

The examiner will share the questions that will be asked. A sample test will be conducted to establish a baseline for the results of the exam. For this preliminary test, you will be instructed to answer "no" to each question, even if doing so would be a lie.

A polygraph is a system which notes the variability of your breathing, sweating, heart rate, and blood pressure. These are the components the examiner assesses. If a person is not telling the truth, there should be an increase in respiratory breathing and heart rate to indicate he or she is telling a lie.

By asking you to answer "no" to questions that are known lies, such as "Have you ever not told the truth to your parents? Have you ever not told the truth to somebody? Have you ever not lied to get out of trouble?" your response will cause a reaction in the polygraph machine, and establish your baseline. The examiner is testing your reaction when you know that you're lying. If someone doesn't react when he or she knows they're lying, then the examiner will be aware that they are a low reactor.

Prior to the actual exam commencing, the examiner will ask again, "Before we begin, is there anything else you would like to say or tell me now before it's too late?" During this entire process, you are also being recorded via video and audio.

The actual length of the polygraph exam is between 15 to 20 minutes, but the entire process can take up to one to two hours.

At the conclusion of the polygraph, the examiner will calculate numbers and inform you that the machine indicates you are being deceptive or truthful. The examiner can tell you anything. If you have been truthful, you have nothing to fear.

The Exit Interview

The completion of the evaluation process is an exit interview. During this meeting you will be asked, "Are you okay? Are you sad? Is there anyone you want to hurt? Do you want to hurt yourself?" This is not a moment to joke or make a light-hearted comment, such as, "Oh my God, I feel like I'm at death's door, and I want to crawl up in a ball and die". Those types of remarks will buy you a 24 to 48-hour hold in the hospital. NO JOKES!

Results: Executive Summary & Recommendation

The executive summary will outline the findings of each area of the evaluation and conclude with a recommendation.

The Executive Summary will be presented by your primary psychologist via a conference call conducted through a secure website. If you haven't yet received the written report, the Executive Summary will be verbalized to you.

The findings may mirror what was found in the investigation or the findings may be incongruent with the investigation and reveal something else. You will be provided a psychological diagnosis based on the evaluation if you have a diagnosis.

POTENTIAL DIAGNOSIS

According to Norman in *The Journal of Medical Regulation*[16], "Disruptive behavior can be manifestations of psychiatric clinical conditions, or personality disorders, or an occasional incident not stemming from underlying psychopathology." A disruptive physician may be diagnosed with:

- Depressive Disorder
- Bipolar Disorder
- Substance Use Disorder
- Attention Deficit Disorder
- Intermittent Explosive Disorder
- Circadian Rhythm Disorder
- Dementia
- Paranoia (pattern of distrust and suspiciousness; such that other's motives are interpreted as malevolent)
- Narcissism (pattern of grandiosity, need for admiration and lack of empathy)
- Passive-aggressive behavior (pattern of negativistic attitudes and passive resistance to demands for adequate performance in social and occupational situations)
- Borderline personality (pattern of instability in interpersonal relationships, self-image, and affects, and marked impulsivity)

The conclusions will note whether you're safe to continue to practice medicine or you're not safe to continue to practice medicine until you successfully complete a course of corrective actions.

There will be a recommendation to send the report, or not, to the Board of Medicine, the Recovery Network and/or somewhere else. The majority of the time, there will be a recommendation of some type of treatment intervention.

It is not the time during the conference call to engage in a conversation. You should simply be listening to the summary, diagnosis and recommendation. Do not try to justify or explain the behavior, or tell the evaluator that he or she made a mistake or is wrong. You may not like the results, but there is no way to appeal the conclusions of the evaluation.

If your goal is to return to work or continue to practice medicine, your mission now is to understand the diagnosis and follow the recommendations so you can achieve your goal.

The results will always include a recommendation that allows you to remedy the situation. If the evaluator feels a physician should not return to work, it is more likely that the recommendation would be something so harsh or punitive that the physician would want to leave rather than completing the corrective action.

Usually, if you complete the recommendations, bring yourself into compliance and correct your behavior, and no longer exhibit or repeat the disruptive behavior, then you can continue to be a doctor and you can continue to work for the hospital. The Medical Executive Committee will have the final approval on your returning to work.

Corrective actions vary and, for example, may be twelve weeks or six weeks of therapy or a three-week professionalism course. This could be outpatient or inpatient. The remedy may be as easy as having a sponsor; someone to talk with on a weekly basis.

According to Reynolds[17], "Professional evaluations yielding individual remediation programs can produce amazingly positive results when they are carefully conducted and there is a good follow-through process, supported by a monitoring program."

"The goal of remediation is improved behavioral functioning. Psychological insight, which rarely occurs, would be a bonus. Educational and other remedies that teach the physician positive coping skills are useful.

According to *The Journal of Medical Regulation*[18], "Remediation should be tailored to the needs of the individual physician based on psychiatric evaluation", and may include:

- Communication skills training
- Anger management
- Negotiation and conflict resolution
- Sensitivity training

- Self-assertiveness training
- Team building
- Impulse control training
- Focused psychotherapy
- Use of psychotropic medications for select cases
- Professionally led assistance groups for physicians with disruptive behavior
- Behavioral coaching
- Assessment utilizing the 360-degree tool
- Periodic psychiatric re-evaluation

Outpatient. Outpatient requires you to seek a therapist who will help you address the issues specific to your situation. The mandated therapy could be weekly, bi-weekly, or monthly, and last five weeks, six-months or three years. It could be individual or group therapy.

Inpatient or Partial Inpatient. Inpatient or Partial Inpatient rehab addresses professionalism and behavior via group interaction as well as private interaction with a therapist. During inpatient or partial inpatient therapy, you will explore why you engage in disruptive behavior and how to change the behavior. You will work alongside other people who are professionals who have encountered similar challenges and will help hold each other accountable.

Recommendations: To Act or Not to Act

Whether you choose to act or not to act on the recommendations of the evaluation will depend on your specific goal. If your goal is to clear your name, then you do it in order to clear your name. If your goal is to stay in your hospital, and you're given the opportunity to complete corrective actions and be reinstated, then you do it. If you say, "No, I'm done with medicine", then you may choose not to complete the recommendations and simply leave the hospital, but understand that this will follow you for the rest of your career. It's not going to go away.

EPILOGUE

MOVING FORWARD:

LEARNING FROM THE EXPERIENCE

Being a part of hospital leadership, I have seen many individuals who have met the title or the description of being "disruptive".

What I've witnessed is that people who are introspective about an accusation are the ones who successfully navigate the remediation process. The people who take it seriously and approach it with an open mind and explore the possibility that they may need to change, are the ones who recover and continue to have fruitful and great careers in healthcare.

The people who deny and become defensive are the ones who have a harder road moving forward. These people are the ones who usually will have the biggest problems. They are not introspective and do not seek self-improvement. These are the physicians who are sent for evaluations or end up leaving hospitals and moving from job to job.

The best advice I can give you in this circumstance is to listen and, even if you don't agree with what is being said, hear it and try to make a change. We like to believe that no one is trying to harm you or be vindictive. Reality is that we do not live in a perfect world and sometimes people are vicious and unkind. I like to believe that people are only trying to help their colleagues.

You can move forward from this experience. You have the choice to either grow from this and leave *shame* behind or let it break you.

RESOURCES

THE DISRUPTIVE PHYSICIAN

www.TheDisruptivePhysician.com

Dr. Jacob DeLaRosa's website, providing additional resources, articles and services related to disruptive behavior for healthcare professionals.

AMERICAN MEDICAL ASSOCIATION

www.ama-assn.org

List of attorneys who specialize in healthcare law.

FEDERATION OF STATE PHYSICIAN HEALTH PROGRAMS

www.fsphp.org

Rehabilitative counseling and behavior modification programs listed by state.

PROFESSIONAL RECOVERY NETWORK

Many states have programs based on the Professional Recovery Network model. Simply do an Internet search of "Professional Recovery Network [+ your state]" for results.

NOTES

1. Reynolds, Norman T. "Disruptive Physician Behavior: Use and Misuse of the Label". *Journal of Medical Regulation*. 2011; Vol 98, No 1: 8

2. Dalco, J. "Disruptive Behavior". *Federation of State Physician Health Programs Physician Health News*. 1999; 3(2): 1-7

3. Horty, John. "When Conduct Crosses the Line". *Medical Staff Monthly*. 1998; 1:3

4. Cohen, B. and Snelson E. "Model Medical Staff Code of Conduct". American Medical Association. 2009

5. Leape, L.L and Fromson, J.A. "Problem Doctors: Is There a System-Level Solution". *Annals of Internal Medicine*. 2006; 144: 104-115

6. Weber, D.O. "For Safety's Sake Disruptive Behavior Must Be Tamed". *Physician Executive*. 2004: 17

7. The Joint Commission. "Behaviors that Undermine a Culture of Safety". *Joint Commission Sentinel Event Alert*. 2008; issue 40

8. Reynolds, Norman T. "Disruptive Physician Behavior: Use and Misuse of the Label". *Journal of Medical Regulation*. 2011; Vol 98, No 1: 13

9. Reynolds, Norman T. "Disruptive Physician Behavior: Use and Misuse of the Label". *Journal of Medical Regulation*. 2011; Vol 98, No 1: 14

10. Reynolds, Norman T. "Disruptive Physician Behavior: Use and Misuse of the Label". *Journal of Medical Regulation*. 2011; Vol 98, No 1: 13

11. American Psychiatric Association. "Passive-Aggressive Personality

Disorder". *Diagnostic and Statistical Manual of Mental Disorders*. 4th edition 1994; 733-735

12. Reynolds, Norman T. "Disruptive Physician Behavior: Use and Misuse of the Label". *Journal of Medical Regulation*. 2011; Vol 98, No 1: 9 (table 1) and 12 (table 6).

13. AMA Healthcare. "Women in Medicine: A Review of Changing Physician Demographics, Female Physicians by Specialty, State and Related Data". *Report/Resource*. 2015; 3 and 9-10

14. Reynolds, Norman T. "Disruptive Physician Behavior: Use and Misuse of the Label". *Journal of Medical Regulation*. 2011; Vol 98, No 1: 15

15. Gregory L. Futral, PhD and James "Jes" Montgomery, MD. "Psychological Assessment Data of Healthcare Professionals Presenting for Evaluation": Poster at Federation of State Physician Health Programs, Inc. Annual Education Conference & Business Meeting. Thursday, April 29, 2016.

16. Reynolds, Norman T. "Disruptive Physician Behavior: Use and Misuse of the Label". *Journal of Medical Regulation*. 2011; Vol 98, No 1: 12 (table 5)

17. Reynolds, Norman T. "Disruptive Physician Behavior: Use and Misuse of the Label". *Journal of Medical Regulation*. 2011; Vol 98, No 1: 15 and Reynolds, Norman T. and Tracy, J. "Case Studies in Evaluating and Managing the Disruptive Physician". *Presentation at the AMA 2000 International Conference on Physician Health*. Seabrook Island, S.C. 200.

18. Reynolds, Norman T. "Disruptive Physician Behavior: Use and Misuse of the Label". *Journal of Medical Regulation*. 2011; Vol 98, No 1: 14 (table 8)

ABOUT THE AUTHOR

Dr. Jacob DeLaRosa is a modern healthcare provider in every sense of the word. He is a dynamic teacher, role model, leader in medicine, celebrity speaker, author and TED talk alumnus.

Dr. DeLaRosa is double board certified in General Surgery and Thoracic surgery. In 2004 he left Emory University and went to Idaho to build the first Cardiothoracic and Endovascular Center in Southeast Idaho.

Suffering from a catastrophic accident while jogging, he was hit by a car doing freeway speed. Since recovering he has focused his efforts on engaging patients and healthcare providers on how positive energy gets you positive results!

His interest in disruptive behaviors began when a colleague was accused of being a "disruptive physician". As a leader in the medical staff, and in the hospital he had never heard of the term, knew what the term meant, or even what it signified. He knew that if he had never heard of the term, that many other physicians, medical staff leaders and administrators hadn't either.

In his extensive research, he found many articles addressing physician disruptive behavior. What was missing was the perspective from a practicing surgeon and what it feels like if you have to go through the process of being termed a disruptive physician.

The book *The Disruptive Physician, How to Manage the Consequences of Being You*, is a step by step guide to avoiding being termed a disruptive physician and if you have already, what to expect.

Learn more at:

www.TheDisruptivePhysician.com

www.HeartSurgeryGamePlan.com

www.ingramcontent.com/pod-product-compliance
Lightning Source LLC
Chambersburg PA
CBHW021343090426
42742CB00008B/719